Grace McHattie

The Cat Maintenance Log Book

With illustrations by John Mansbridge

Methuen · London

By the same author

The Cat Maintenance Manual

First published in Great Britain 1986
by Methuen London Ltd
11 New Fetter Lane, London EC4P 4EE
Text © 1986 Grace McHattie
Illustrations © 1986 John Mansbridge
Reproduced, printed and bound
in Great Britain

British Library Cataloguing in Publication Data

McHattie, Grace
   The cat maintenance log book
   1. Cats
   I. Title
   636.8'083   SF447

   ISBN 0–413–14450–X

Cat or kitten's name: _____KINCADE_____

Address: _____194, CHALVEY GROVE_____

_____SLOUGH_____

_____BERKSHIRE_____

Date of birth: _____JUNE 26TH_____

Breed or type: _____TABBY_____

Colour(s): _____TYPICAL TABBY_____

Sex: _____MALE_____

Longhair or shorthair: _____SHORT_____

Any distinguishing
markings: _____DEFORMED RIGHT HIND LEG._____

Note your
cat's
markings here

Use this record as a complete description of your cat, in case he ever goes missing. It's much easier to write a full description beforehand, when your cat is with you, than if you are upset about a missing pet. Make sure you have at least one clear, good-quality photograph of your pet – glue it by the corners onto the page overleaf. If you ever have to advertise to find your cat, the photograph can be used on posters and will prove extremely useful.

Favourite Feline Photos

Paste photo here

Paste photo here

Address Cat-a-log

Cats Protection League: local branches throughout the UK rescue and rehome strays. Write to 17 Kings Road, Horsham, West Sussex RH13 5PP for the address of the one nearest to you, if you can help or give a cat a home.

Cinnamon Trust: runs a sanctuary to care for the pets of elderly owners who have to enter a home or hospital, or for owners who die. 68 Carn Brea Lane, Pool, Redruth, Cornwall TR15 3DS.

Charities Aid Foundation: has produced a directory of animal welfare organisations, details from 48 Pembury Road, Tonbridge, Kent.

Feline Advisory Bureau: has a boarding cattery approval service. FAB also funds a scholarship for a vet to work in the only specialist feline consultancy for cats in the UK at Langford, University of Bristol. All vets can refer difficult cases there. 350 Upper Richmond Road, London SW15 6TL.

People's Dispensary for Sick Animals: runs local veterinary surgeries where animals can be treated at low cost, or free of charge, if their owners cannot afford private veterinary treatment. South Street, Dorking, Surrey RH4 2LB.

Petwatch: runs a nationwide network of missing pets bureaux. PO Box 16, Brighouse, West Yorkshire HD6 1DS.

Royal Society for the Prevention of Cruelty to Animals: trains and employs inspectors who investigate cruelty and neglect. The RSPCA also runs many animal homes throughout the UK. The Causeway, Horsham, West Sussex RH12 1HQ.

St Andrew Animal Fund: as well as the protection of animals and their humane treatment, the fund wish to popularise local, low-cost spaying and neutering clinics. 10 Queensferry Street, Edinburgh EH2 4PQ.

The Governing Council of the Cat Fancy: is the longest-established registration organisation for pedigree cats and holds many shows for pedigree and non-pedigree cats each year. 4–6 Penel Orlieu, Bridgwater, Somerset.

The Cat Association: formed in 1983, this is also a registration organisation which holds shows for pedigree and non-pedigree cats. Hunting Grove, Lowfield Heath, Crawley, West Sussex.

The Independent Pet Cat Society: formed in 1985, the IPCS holds cat shows for 'pet-quality' pedigree cats and non-pedigree cats. 105 Culvers Way, Carshalton, Surrey SM5 2LN.

Cat World: a monthly magazine covering all cat topics. Scan House, Southwick Street, Southwick, Brighton BN4 4TE.

Inoculation Record

Feline Panleucopenia (Feline Enteritis) _____

_____

Feline Viral Rhinotracheitis _____

_____

Feline Calici Virus _____

_____

1st dose _____ 2nd dose _____

_____

Booster due each _____

Having your cat vaccinated regularly will protect him from several potentially
fatal diseases. Kittens are usually given a triple vaccine around the age of
three or four months. Check with your vet – they all have their own ideas
about when the first injection can be given. It will be followed with a second
vaccination about three to six weeks later, and a booster will be given once a
year. As well as protecting your cat's health, current certificates of
vaccination are required before a reputable cattery will accept him as a
boarder, or before he can enter a cat show.

Worming Record

Date	Treatment
_____	_____
_____	_____
_____	_____
_____	_____

Kittens and cats should be regularly wormed with a roundworm preparation.
Ask your vet's advice on frequency of worming. Although roundworms are
the most common type of worm a cat may harbour, there are several other
types which can only be treated with specific preparations from your vet.

Veterinary Record

Vet's name: _____

Address: _____

_____

Phone no.: _____

Date	Diagnosis	Treatment

Should your cat require an operation or a course of treatment for an illness, veterinary costs can quickly mount. You can cushion the effects of this by taking out pet health insurance. There are many different companies which offer insurance (they usually advertise in veterinary surgeries) and their schemes should be carefully compared before a decision is made. Some schemes cost appreciably more than others, without giving correspondingly more cover. No policy will cover the cost of routine treatment such as vaccinations, neutering or any condition associated with breeding. Some schemes will reimburse the amount paid for your cat should he die and some will pay boarding fees for your cat should *you* become hospitalised. The best time to take out a policy is when your cat is young and healthy – many schemes will exclude treatment for an illness from which a cat has already suffered and many companies will not accept previously-uninsured animals over the age of eight or ten.

Family Tree

Timely Warnings

Spring

If your cat is spending more time indoors during wet spring weather, he'll be expending some of his energy in play. Do ensure that his playthings are safe. Cats love to chase string but string can be deadly if left lying around. Cats have rasp-like tongues and, if they get string into their mouths, it's easier for them to swallow it than to spit it out. Swallowed string can knot up or perforate the intestines and major surgery may be required to remove it. Many cats enjoy chasing rolled-up balls of paper. These should be made much too large to swallow. Wind-up toys and other children's toys also make good playthings for cats but do make sure they are large and have no sharp corners or small pieces which might break off. Catnip toys, made specially for cats, are safe as long as you don't allow your cat out of doors within half an hour or so of playing with them. It takes that time for the sense-dulling effect to wear off.

And in the garden, if you're clearing the winter's dead wood, do make sure your cat is shut in the house before you start pruning. Many cats are fascinated by the flashing shears and can put out their paws to 'play' with them – with disastrous consequences. Also, before lighting a bonfire, make sure your cat is indoors. The inside of an unlit bonfire is often a favourite hiding-place.

Summer

Summer brings many problems for the cat-loving gardener. Unfortunately, cats are much more susceptible to poisons than many other animals, and insecticides and weedkillers in common use are often very toxic to cats.

There is really only one way of weeding which is guaranteed not to cause problems for your cats, and that is to pull the weeds out by hand. Many garden chemicals state they are not toxic to pets if used as directed. Where cats are concerned, they should be used with even more care than the manufacturer recommends. For example, weedkillers to be used on paths often state on the packet that pets should be kept indoors until the area has dried. If you have no option but to use this sort of product, you should take the instruction to mean that – in the very driest weather – you should keep cats off them for 24 hours at the very least. Remember that the following morning, the area may be damp again following the night's dew. Insecticides should all be used with the greatest care. It might be better to plant together plants which discourage pests – onions beside carrots, for example – and to encourage ladybirds and spiders to live in your garden! Slug pellets are highly poisonous to cats. As they are often bran-based, cats will eat them. If you have to use them, place them underneath an upturned flowerpot. The slugs will be able to eat them but your cat won't.

Any suspected garden poisoning should be immediately treated by a vet, as should any bee or wasp stings in the region of the nose or mouth.

Autumn

The cat's susceptibility to toxic substances extends into the home. Use antiseptics with care (see page 55) and also be careful about the disinfectants and cleansers you use. For example, many of the products used to clean kitchen floors and work surfaces could make your cat ill if he walks on them while still wet. The safest disinfectant to use (which can also be used as a cleanser) is a weak solution of sodium hypochlorite in water, ie. Domestos and similar products. This is also the best solution to use for sterilising your cat's feeding and water bowls and his litter tray. Cats will often refuse to use a tray which has been cleaned with a pine-scented disinfectant.

Cats are very inquisitive creatures so you should try to make your home as safe as you can for him. Many cats will investigate inside washing-machines and dishwashers as they are being filled. Always check your cat isn't inside before you switch on.

If you live in a flat, don't open the windows more than two inches unless you have a wire screen to fit over the opening. Many people think their cats are too clever to fall out, but every year cats are severely injured or even killed by chasing insects straight out of the window.

Another thing to be careful of, especially with young kittens, is to keep the loo seat-cover down! Many kittens have fallen inside, only to find they can't climb out again because of the slippery surface.

Winter

Winter can have its share of hazards for cats. Your cat should be spending his nights indoors anyway, but this is particularly important on cold, dark winter nights. Make sure he has a warm bed indoors. Some cats, such as the short-coated Rex, can suffer from hypothermia, even indoors, in particularly cold weather and should have a warm blanket to snuggle under, or night-time heating.

If changing the anti-freeze in your car, dispose of the anti-freeze carefully and mop up any spills. Ethylene glycol is a common anti-freeze ingredient and has a taste which is attractive to cats, yet it is highly poisonous. If swallowed, it will make your cat sick and can cause convulsions or unconsciousness.

Christmas poses particular problems. Cats simply will not leave Christmas trees alone, so only decorate yours with large, unbreakable ornaments – no glass ornaments which will shatter and cause cut paws, and nothing small enough to swallow. Tinsel often attracts cats and, if they start to nibble it, may find themselves swallowing large amounts, with terrible consequences. If your cat nibbles electric wires, either don't have lights on your tree, or else protect any reachable wire in plastic tubing. The Christmas tree itself can pose problems if it is a real one. Shed pine needles can be swallowed causing serious sickness. And remember that mistletoe and holly are poisonous to cats.

If you're having a Christmas party or relatives visiting, your cat will probably appreciate being shut away from the noise in a quiet room with his litter tray, a few safe toys and *his* Christmas dinner!

Breed Cat-a-Log

If buying a cat, choose one whose personality and temperament will suit you and the life you lead. Most cats are bought solely on their looks, which can be a great mistake. The most popular breeds are the demanding Siamese and the time-consuming Persian, neither of which may be the ideal cat for the average busy owner. Although each cat is an individual, the various breeds have very distinct personalities.

Abyssinian: Abys are ideal cats for people who live alone. One-person cats, they will give their owners a great deal of love and companionship. They like company and a stay-at-home owner would be ideal for them.

Angora: Angoras would also be happier with non-working owners as they enjoy company and admiration. They want to be the centre of attention and are affectionate and even-tempered. They don't need to be groomed daily, as their coat is finer than the Persian. They're good cats for flat-dwellers.

Balinese: These are basically longhaired Siamese which have been developed into a separate breed. In temperament, they are very similar to the Siamese although not quite so noisy! Their long coat is silky, so rarely matts and they don't shed much.

Birman: Daily grooming of the Birman's long cream coat is essential although they shed less than Persians. They are companionable cats, becoming very devoted to their owners and often following them around. They're even-tempered and can keep themselves occupied while an owner is at work.

British (and American) shorthair: These are catty cats; independent yet affectionate, intelligent, gentle and lovable. They are sturdy, healthy and resilient and make rewarding pets. Grooming is simple.

Burmese: Excellent pets for anyone with a busy lifestyle, these cats are adaptable and independent with fascinating characters. They are solidly-built, healthy cats and can be very friendly when they want to be! They can be vocal, but not to the same extent as the Siamese.

Chinchilla: These can make ideal one-person cats and would probably be happiest in a one-person household. They can be very sensitive and some don't like much handling, so they're not ideal if you have children. They will live happily in a flat but their long white fur needs daily attention and moulting could irritate the houseproud!

Colourpoint (Himalayan): They are less demanding and noisy than the Siamese but they do enjoy attention and make sure they get it. They are affectionate and devoted and enjoy family life, liking a degree of liberty and a garden for play. Daily grooming is necessary.

Foreign: Foreign Whites, Lilacs and Blacks are related to the Siamese. Consequently their temperament is similar, but quieter. They are real characters and appreciate owners who will allow them free range for their strong personalities.

Maine Coon: These are healthy, hardy cats, sociable and playful. They are devoted to their owners but are highly intelligent and independent. They are big, heavy cats and would want a garden for play. Their coats are silky, so grooming is easy.

Non-Pedigree: The non-pedigree cat would probably fit in best with a busy owner's lifestyle. Their characters will vary according to their parentage but usually they are healthy, hardy and independent. They're more 'street-wise' than the average pedigree cat and tend to be more resistant to infection. Don't buy the kittens from pet shops, where nothing will be known about their backgrounds and where they may have been living in stressful or unhealthy situations. Try to see the kitten's mother and gauge her health and temperament – dad's too, if he's known!

Persian: These are probably the most difficult cats to groom. Don't consider buying one unless you are prepared to brush him (often against his will) for at least ten minutes *every* day. They also shed hair heavily. They're renowned for their sweet, placid nature and are real 'lap cats'. They are affectionate and loving and won't mind living in a flat.

Rex: Cornish and Devon Rex are bold and adventurous, intelligent and extremely (almost hyper-) active. They always want to be with their owners and are very people-orientated – and greedy. Their big ears need weekly cleaning and, unfortunately, their waste products are particularly smelly! *Some* people who suffer a mild allergic reaction to cats may not with a Rex, probably because of their short coats. Although interesting and unique cats, many people might find them hard-going as pets.

Russian Blue: These cats have sweet temperaments and quiet natures and are friendly but not demanding. They are independent and adaptable and enjoy family life, being equally friendly with children and other pets. Grooming is sufficient once-weekly.

Siamese: Siamese are quite a handful, being demanding and extremely noisy and they insist on a large proportion of their owner's time and attention. They love to claw and should always be provided with a scratching-post. They like to climb, especially curtains, so if your furniture is precious to you, you should consider another breed. They are extroverted 'show offs' and very inquisitive. They're also highly intelligent and can be trained, to walk on a leash, for example. They like to have another cat for company.

Somali: These cats are bright, alert and nosy! They want to investigate everything and are lively cats who love to romp and play. They are bold and don't mind dogs and usually love children. They are strong and healthy and can become very devoted to their owners. Grooming is simple and an occasional brushing is sufficient.

Turkish Van: These are very accommodating cats who will fit in well in any family situation and won't mind dogs. Don't buy one if you have a canary, though – they're great hunters! They enjoy attention and will steal small items and retrieve balls thrown by their owners. They can amuse themselves while an owner is at work and they love water, in which they will splash around and play. They do need daily grooming and shedding in spring is quite heavy.

If you're thinking of picking up some January sale bargains, bear in mind your cat's preferences – it'll make life easier for you both!

If you are buying a television set or video-recorder, those with remote-control devices *can* annoy and upset cats. Most remote-control devices work by infra-red, which won't cause problems, but if the remote-control device works ultra-sonically, your cat will be able to hear the high-pitched sound it makes and this can cause him distress.

A new microwave oven can frighten a cat when it pings to show that the cooking time is finished. The first meal you cook in your microwave should be a plate of tasty fish for your cat and you'll have no problems!

If buying new carpets, keep your cats off them for the first weeks or even months until all the loose fluff and fibre has been vacuumed up. They could inhale or swallow the fluff with serious consequences. Carpets which have been given a water- or dirt-proofing treatment can cause an allergic reaction in cats. The chemical used can be an eye irritant, giving a cat runny or sore eyes.

Cats love to scratch and climb, so curtains and upholstery fabric in open weaves or rough textures will tempt them. Smooth or shiny fabrics will last longer in a 'catty' home! Hessian wallpaper also tends to tatter very quickly as most cats will literally use it to climb the walls.

Wickerwork chairs and linen baskets will be used enthusiastically for claw-sharpening, so it's best to steer clear of these too; but perhaps you'll find a scratching-post – or a carpet offcut to make one – in the sales to keep everyone happy.

January

1

2

3

4

5

You can stop your cat digging up your pot plants by covering the soil with a piece of plastic. Or cut wire mesh into a circle the same size as the pot top, snipping it open along the radius, to allow you to slip it around the plant.

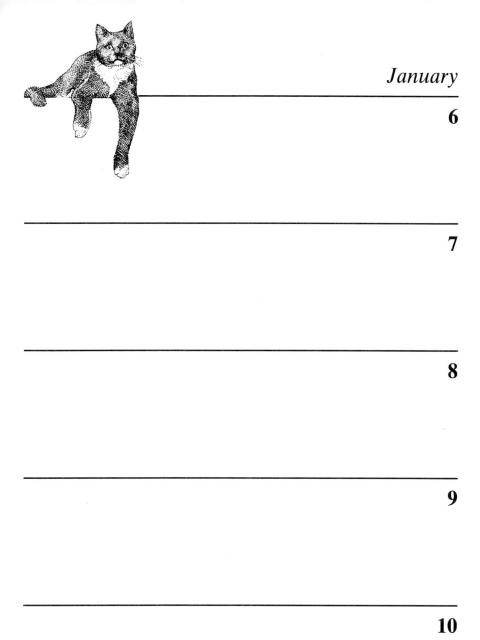

January

6

7

8

9

10

January

11

12

13

14

15

16

17

18

A large washing-up bowl
makes a cheap and
cheerful litter tray. Its
depth allows a deeper
layer of litter to be used
and your cat is less likely
to scatter litter around
when 'covering up' in a
deep bowl.

19

20

January

21

It's easier to give pills to a
cat when you gently
restrain him first by
wrapping him in a towel.
After you've dropped the
pill on the back of the
tongue, you can make him
swallow by stroking his
throat or touching his nose.

22

23

24

25

January

26

27

28

29

30

31

February

If you're going away on a summer holiday, *now* is the time to book a boarding cattery for your cat, as the best catteries are booked up very early in the year.

You can acquire a list of approved catteries from the Feline Advisory Bureau, or pick one out of your local telephone directory. It is important that you should thoroughly inspect the cattery before making a booking and ensure that you see all over the premises – sometimes substandard accommodation is hidden away.

Make sure the cattery is clean with no unpleasant smells. The boarders should look happy and healthy. The people in charge should be interested in your cat and his individual preferences.

Cats are prone to very serious respiratory infections, often spread by sneezes, so runs or chalets should be spaced out with impermeable barriers between. Cats cannot safely be housed in cages which are sometimes stacked close together in tiers.

Runs and chalets should have inner *and* outer doors as many cats will try to escape their confinement. Every reputable cattery owner will expect your cat to have current vaccinations and will insist on seeing certificates of vaccination.

Your local newspaper may carry an advertisement for a 'cat-sitting' service, where someone will come to your home once or twice a day to feed and look after your cats. If you have more than one cat, this service may work out less expensive than a cattery, and it will be a less traumatic experience for some cats, who hate to have their routine interrupted. Be sure to interview your cat-sitter and ask for references. Ensure you leave a full written list of your cat's preferences, diet and routine – and the name and phone number of your vet, as well as a number where you can be contacted.

February

1

2

3

4

5

February

6

7

8

9

10

11

12

13

14

Valentine's Day! Show
your cat you love him by
making him a catnip heart.
Cut two pieces of strong
fabric in a heart shape and
hem wrong sides leaving a
small space unstitched.
Turn, stuff with catnip, and
sew up remaining edge.

15

February

16

17

Change a cat's food gradually,
perhaps mixing his new food with
what he's used to. Otherwise,
tummy upsets may result. It's very
important for a cat to have a varied
diet; for example, liver (high in
Vitamin A) fed more than once or
twice a week, could make your cat
very ill.

18

19

20

February

21

22

23

24

25

February

26

27

28

29

March

Wet March days may mean that your cat is staying indoors more and not getting enough exercise. If you're being woken at 5 a.m. by an energetic cat, you'll want to dissipate some of that energy during the daytime.

By playing with your cat for just ten or so minutes regularly each day, you will ensure his heart and blood vessels will stay strong and healthy, increase his stamina, reduce stress (and so raise his resistance against many diseases) and alleviate the boredom which can lead to stress-related 'destructive' behaviour. Young cats have an almost insatiable capacity for play and older cats will have their muscles toned, their breathing improved and their appetites sharpened by a gentle exercise period each day.

Start gently with a few minutes' warm-up exercises and have a 'cooling-down' period at the end. Exercise at the same time each day, not too near mealtimes.

Hang a sturdy rope from a piece of furniture so that it dangles free of the floor. Bat it towards your cat and he'll usually start playing with it.

Cats, especially those not allowed out of doors, love to stalk and chase things. Trail a piece of rope for them, or a long stick or piece of twig, or a tall feather. Or you can make a 'fishing-rod' using a cane with string firmly attached and a piece of tough fabric on the end as 'bait'. This will give your cat plenty of exercise while you sit in your chair.

Of course, cats love to chase and bat things around. Table-tennis balls or golf practice balls (plastic balls with holes in them) are particularly good and cats also enjoy toys which roll erratically. Let yours play with empty plastic lemons, walnuts, pine cones, wine corks, plastic eggs from fairgrounds, empty thread spools or plastic drinking cups.

March

1

2

3

4

5

March

6

7

8

9

10

To deter a cat from scratching
a fabric, rinse it in vinegar,
lemon juice or peppermint
oil, or dab it with Tabasco
sauce (check it doesn't stain
the fabric). Or cover the
fabric with plastic – cats hate
the feel of it under their paws.

March

11

12

13

Brush or comb your cat regularly,
especially in the spring, or if he's
elderly and can't quite manage it
himself. This will help keep hairs
on your furniture to a minimum
and stop your cat swallowing hair
which can form into furballs in his
stomach. Apart from which, it's a
friendly thing to do!

14

15

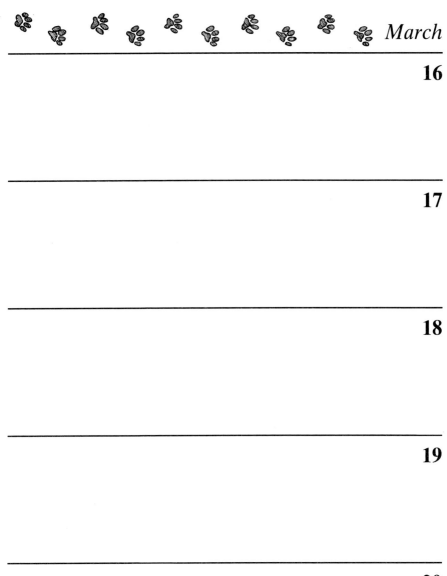

16

17

18

19

20

March

21

22

23

24

25

March

26

Make sure your cat always has fresh water to drink – it's important for his health. Some cats prefer to drink from dripping taps, while some will only drink water from their bowls when the chlorinated smell has dispersed. Don't worry if your cat won't drink milk – he doesn't need it if he has plenty of water and a good diet.

27

28

29

30

31

April

The flea 'season' begins with the onset of warmer weather, although in centrally-heated homes they can be a year-round problem. You can tell your cat has fleas if, when you brush him, the groomings contain tiny white eggs or little dark specks. You will see these easily if you brush your cat while he is standing on a white cloth or paper. Scratching, usually around the neck or face, is another sign of the presence of fleas.

There are many preparations which can help get rid of fleas. Those bought from a vet have the most powerful active constituents. Sprays and powders which will kill fleas are, obviously, strong-acting – and can prove toxic to cats if the greatest care is not taken in their use. It's vital that a cat should not inhale spray or powder, nor should he be sprayed in the room where his feeding and water bowls are. If possible, spray your cat out of doors, ensuring that spray is blowing away from your cat's face. After a few minutes, brush out his coat. Flea collars release a powdered insecticide which spreads over a cat's coat. A collar should be taken off for a few hours each day, or if it becomes wet, or if your cat has an allergic reaction to it.

It's possible to buy sprays which will kill or inhibit the growth of fleas in their breeding areas and it will be necessary to spray these around your home as well as using a separate flea treatment on your cat if the infestation is bad.

It's now possible to buy herbal flea collars and other treatments – they're advertised in cat magazines. Or you could try this herbal deterrent; pour boiling water over cut-up lemon pieces and leave to infuse for several days. Rub the resulting lotion into your cat's coat.

Or you can simply comb your cat thoroughly and regularly with a flea comb, picking out fleas and drowning or burning them!

1

2

3

4

5

April

6

7

8

9

When you have a new kitten
which hasn't yet been out of
doors, make sure you don't
open any windows more
than an inch or so.
Adventurous young kittens
can squeeze through a gap of
only two inches.

10

11

12

13

14

15

April

16

17

18

19

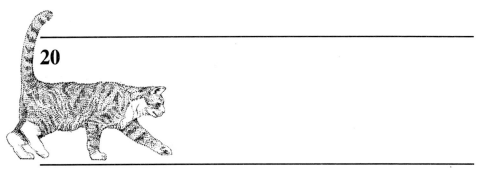

20

21

22

It's a fallacy that a cat should have one litter before being spayed. Spayed cats have no maternal instincts and don't miss what they've never had. Pregnancy can be uncomfortable and painful for them and you'll be adding to the numbers of unwanted cats – or preventing another cat from finding a home – by letting your cat have a litter.

23

24

25

April

26

27

28

29

30

May

To give your cat a year-round treat, plant catnip now. Catnip (*Nepeta cataria*), also called catmint, is an aromatic herb which most cats love, although a few are indifferent to it. It can be grown indoors in a pot or transplanted out of doors in late May or June. The plant likes sun and grows best in poor soil, doing particularly well in chalky soil.

It will take about ten days for the seeds to germinate. When transplanting, be careful not to damage the leaves as this will bruise them, releasing the smell and attracting cats from a wide area! Garden catnip plants will have to be protected with wire mesh, or upended lampshade frames, as cats may otherwise nibble the leaves as they appear. Whitish flowers will appear in July or August and the plants should be picked on a sunny morning before the flower buds open. Hang the plants in small bunches in a warm, airy room, away from sunlight. Drying should be complete in about a week or ten days. Crumble the leaves and store in glass containers or plastic bags for future use.

Catnip has many uses. It relaxes cats and they will nibble it, roll ecstatically in it and enjoy playing with toys containing catnip. If rubbed on a scratching-post, or sprinkled in a litter tray, it will encourage cats to use them. A cat visiting the vet will feel happier in his basket if a little catnip has been sprinkled there first. If you want to photograph your cat and he won't stay still, a sprinkle of catnip should help keep him in position for the camera.

The active component of catnip is nepetalactone, which works on the cat's nervous system. It is important, if catnip is used, that your cat be given time to return to normal before being allowed outside again. So remember – don't let him outdoors for a least half an hour after playing with anything containing catnip.

May

1

2

3

4

5

If a cat is doing something you don't
want him to do, a squirt of clean
water from a water pistol will
usually discourage him, without
him realising you are the person
'punishing' him! Or use a very
thoroughly washed-out squeezy
bottle instead.

6

7

8

9

10

May

11

12

13

14

15

May

16

17

18

Some cats will 'ambush' their owners, leaping out and scratching or biting. This isn't naughtiness but over-boisterous play. You can channel this energy into less-painful areas by carrying a small toy or ball around with you. If your cat 'attacks' you, immediately drop the toy and transfer your cat's attention to that instead.

19

20

May

21

Some young kittens insist on sucking the
bare skin of their new owners. Check he's
not hungry or thirsty (kittens should have
four meals a day until up to about six
months) and if he persists, paint a nail-
biting solution on your skin to discourage
him. Or use vinegar on your skin. You'll
smell like a chip but the kitten won't like it
either!

22

23

24

25

26

27

28

29

30

31

June

With the advent of warm weather and gardeners cutting their grass, the number of missing cats rises! The reason is that cats, being curious, love to investigate open garden sheds and then get locked in. So get to know the boundaries of your cat's territory, and, if he goes missing, look first in the closed sheds in the area.

If this fails, you should have a complete description of your cat on page 3 and a clear photograph on page 4. Use these to make up a 'missing' poster and photocopy for distribution. Put the posters through your neighbours' letterboxes and display them in local shop windows and at your vet's surgery.

Phone all the vets in the area – your cat may have been injured and taken to any veterinary surgery. Contact your local police station; although not obliged to keep records of lost and found cats, many officers can be very helpful. Advertise in the 'lost and found' section of your local newspaper. Contact your local radio station.

Contact any welfare organisations in your area; not just the major ones. Keep in touch with these organisations and call them several times a week – often they're too busy to call you.

If you've recently moved home, get in touch with the occupants at your old address. Ask your neighbours if they had deliveries being made at the time your cat went missing. Many lost cats 'stow away' in furniture or delivery vans, then run off in fright when the van stops. If you can discover from the firm where the van stopped, you could search in that area. You can also contact the charity Petwatch, which runs a nationwide network of missing pets bureaux (see page 5).

With luck, you will find your cat – so do be sure to tell all the people you have contacted that he is home, safe and sound.

1

2

3

4

5

June

6

7

8

9

10

11

12

13

14

Don't use fly strips or blocks
which are sometimes placed on
floors to kill fleas. They can
cause toxicity in cats and are
particularly dangerous if you've
already sprayed your cat or if he
wears a flea collar, as he can
suffer an overdose of the active
ingredient.

15

June

16

17

If you buy a new cat or kitten, take your
carrying basket into his home and open it.
Let him and his litter-mates play in and out
of it. When it's time to leave, it will smell
familiar to him and he will accept his
temporary confinement more readily.
Place a pinch of catnip in the basket to
make it a pleasant place to be.

18

19

20

21

22

23

24

25

June

26

27

28

29

30

July

Long summer days will mean that your cat spends more time out of doors. If any minor accidents should befall him, you should know a few elementary first aid tips.

A cat's ears are very vulnerable. Cut ears – or any other part of the body – should *not* be treated with certain antiseptics. Those which contain chlorinated phenols are toxic to cats. Be alert for any signs of infection – in which case a visit to the vet is essential. Head-shaking or ear-scratching may mean that ear mites are present, in which case your vet should treat the problem, or it may mean that a grass seed-head has found its way into the ear. If you can see it, put a little soapy water (don't use detergent) in the ear. If this doesn't flush it out, your vet should be asked to deal with it.

These seed-heads might also lodge in your cat's eye, in which case, plain water may flush it out. Sometimes a thorn can become embedded in a cat's eye, or a fight injury may cause a problem. Usually a white speck is visible in the eye and this will need veterinary attention. If this is not immediately available, short-term first aid can consist of a drop of olive or cooking oil dripped into the eye to lubricate it, until the vet is available.

For cuts or grazes which are not serious, an application of salty water (one teaspoon of salt in a pint of water) can be made and care should be taken that the injury doesn't become infected. Injured paws can be dipped in a cup of salty water.

A cat with a broken limb should be carried with one hand holding the scruff of the neck while the other supports the chest. An unconscious cat should be carried to the vet on a jacket or coat.

Whatever the injury, never give a cat aspirin or paracetamol, which is so toxic to cats that it may kill them. And if in any doubt, do see your vet.

July

1

2

3

4

5

6

7

8

9

10

It isn't true that cats are smelly!
Well-cared-for cats aren't. Males
should be neutered, then they are
less likely to mark their territory
with their pungent-smelling urine –
unless too many cats are kept in too
small a space. Four is often the
danger number.

11

12

13

Most cats don't like flea sprays – the hissing
noise they make sounds like an angry cat to
them. You can apply flea powder by puffing it
into an old pillowcase. Put your cat inside with
his head clear and gently hold the bag around
his neck. Massage the powder into his fur
through the bag. Take him out and brush out
any remaining powder.

14

15

16

17

18

19

20

July

21

22

23

24

25

26

Many cats will learn to walk on a leash. Start
training by accustoming your cat to a collar
(without a lead attached), then a special cat
harness, which should be used with the lead –
cats will slip out of an ordinary collar. Practise
in a garden first and let your cat walk where he
likes. Later he can learn to walk where you
want him to by rewarding him with treats.

27

28

29

30

31

August

An understanding of body language is considered important even in the human world. It's much more important when you are dealing with a creature which has no other way of communicating.

A happy cat will purr; it's considered to be the equivalent of the human smile. The rougher the purr sounds, the happier your cat is feeling. (Though purring can be a warning signal too; if a sick or injured cat begins to purr, it's a sign he's in pain.) Sometimes, the happy purr will be accompanied by your cat kneading his paws against your skin. Unfortunately, this can be painful for the owner but it simply means the cat is blissfully happy, so is difficult to discourage. The behaviour stems from kittenhood when the kneading action stimulated the mother's milk. The happy cat will also carry his head and ears high and his tail will be straight up in the air. When in a very good mood, your cat will curl the tip of his tail over his back.

Ears are an excellent indication of your cat's mood; he's happy if his ears are upright, ecstatic if his ears point forward. Ears flattened sideways are the sign of a defensive cat, while ears flattened backwards are the sign of a cat considering attack.

A wagging tail means your cat is alert, while a thrashing tail is a sign of anger.

If his eyes are half-closed, he's either anxious or he's telling you he loves you. Quick blinks are a sign of nervousness, as is rapid lip-licking.

It has been calculated that cats use approximately sixteen spoken phrases, each with a distinct and different meaning. Many of these have, in fact, been developed for the benefit of humans, who quickly learn the commands for food and door-opening!

1

2

3

4

5

August

6

7

8

9

Goldfish-owning cat lovers
won't need to be reminded to
keep their fish tanks covered.
But when using a flea
treatment on your cat, don't
spray him in the room where
the fish tank is housed. Flea
spray can kill fish.

10

11

12

13

14

15

August

16

17

18

19

20

21

22

The occasional tear-stain on
your cat's face can be wiped
off with a piece of cotton
wool squeezed out in a weak
solution of boric acid
(available from chemists) and
water. Or use cotton wool
squeezed out in a weak
solution of cold tea.

23

24

25

August

26

27

28

29

30

31

September

With longer nights and wetter weather, your cat will be grateful for the use of an indoor 'bathroom'. Providing him with a litter tray will make his life much more comfortable.

There are several types of litter tray, including the inexpensive basic tray available from most pet shops. There are also covered trays: the tray has a covered plastic 'tent' with an entrance door. This type of tray keeps your home cleaner as your cat won't scatter the litter outside, and many cats like them as they prefer privacy. There is even a litter tray which comes with re-usable, washable litter!

Most cat litter is of mineral origin. It is natural clay which is mined, dried and the dust removed, without any additives. There are two types of lightweight white litter, usually imported from Spain or Africa, and a pinkish-brown litter from Denmark. The most used type of litter is the grey Fullers' Earth, mined in Britain. It is usually less expensive than other mineral litters and neutralises ammonia.

There are also litters made from pine and coniferous wood. The wood is crushed, the dust extracted, then it is dried and pelletised. It is highly absorbent and, as it is bio-degradable, the used litter can be burnt, buried or placed on the compost heap.

If you are changing from one type of litter to another, your cat may resist at first. If so, place a fine layer of your old litter on top of the new.

Mineral litters are most economical if used in a depth of two or three inches. The litter will 'clump' when wet and the wet ball can be easily lifted out. The pelletised softwood litters should be used in a depth of about an inch as the wood expands when wet.

September

1

2

3

4

5

If you have an electric cooker,
the cooking rings will stay hot
for a long time after you've
turned them off. If your cat
jumps onto them, he'll be badly
burned. Keep them covered – or,
better still, keep your cat out of
the kitchen during, and just after,
cooking.

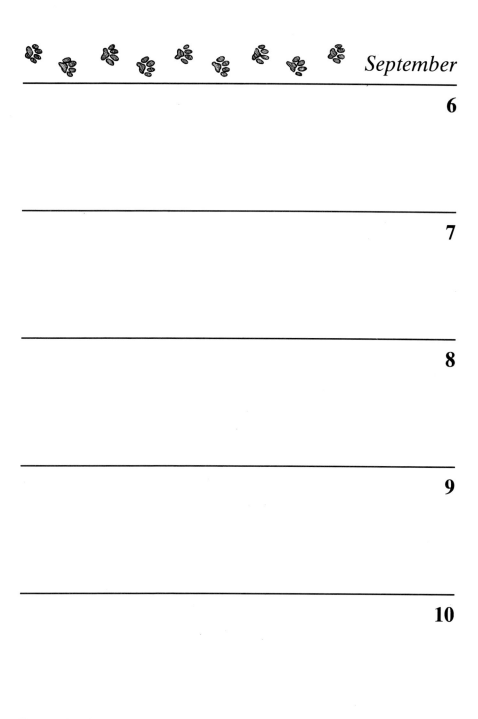

September

6

7

8

9

10

September

11

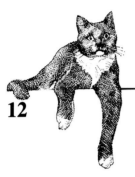

12

13

14

15

September

16

17

18

Don't 'put the cat out' all
night: he'll be cold and
miserable, get into fights and
may be run over or stolen.
Make sure your cat is used to
staying indoors at night from
an early age and give him a
cosy bed and a litter tray.

19

20

September

21

Don't waste fat trimmings
(cooked or raw) from meat or
chops. Cats love additional fat
and, as they have a high fat
requirement, it will do them no
harm. And you could give your
cat an occasional egg yolk (not
the white). It's very nutritious and
most cats love it.

22

23

24

25

26

27

28

29

30

October

Some people believe it's a waste of time to buy a cat bed as they are convinced their cat will always sleep on their favourite armchair anyway! Modern cat beds are so varied in design and so comfortable that most cats will use them in preference to the fireside rug.

Remember to take your cat's preferences into account when buying a bed. Some cats like to sleep stretched out, in which case you'll have to buy a bigger bed than for a cat which sleeps curled up.

Most beds have high sides which will help keep your cat cosy and out of draughts. Some 'igloo' types have hooded tops and these are often popular, although some cats will take several days to get used to the idea. In a household with more than one cat, these beds are often treated with suspicion as one cat may hide inside it to ambush the others!

All modern beds are completely washable (an important point as beds can harbour fleas) and the deluxe models have fur linings, which is particularly cosy and comfortable for the older cat.

There are many beanbags for cats and these are very cosy as the filling conducts heat around all parts of the body in contact with it. They are machine-washable and won't harbour fleas. However, some cats become confused; the filling sounds and feels like cat litter under the paws – so they use them as lavatories! If you have a cat who is easily confused, you'd be better buying him a different sort of bed.

Location of the bed is important. It should be in a draught-free place, away from the main traffic areas. Many cats like to sleep high up, feeling more secure that way, and some are happiest if their bed is placed on top of a cupboard or wardrobe.

1

2

3

4

5

October

6

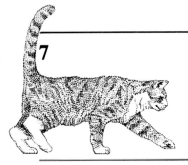

7

8

9

10

October

11

12

13

14

Don't use a wall-mounted tin-
opener for opening tins of cat
food. It's difficult to wash
thoroughly after use and
contamination can be passed on
to human food from tins of cat
food. Always keep a separate
tin-opener to be used
exclusively for cat food.

15

October

16

17

If your cat won't use his litter
tray, make sure it's kept clean –
cats won't use a smelly tray.
Perhaps he doesn't like the
disinfectant you use or the type
of litter. You should have one
tray per cat and keep it in a
quiet and private place!

18

19

20

October

21

22

23

24

25

October

26

27

28

29

30

31

November

If you've ever thought your cat was a winner, now is your chance to prove it as the show season gets under way.

Almost every cat show has a non-pedigree section and some shows are held *only* for non-pedigree cats, so you don't need to own an expensive pedigree to have the thrill of a winning cat. Although pedigree cats are judged according to the 'standard of points' (a list of attributes of the 'perfect' cat of that breed), non-pedigree cats are judged on health, condition and temperament.

A nervous or bad-tempered cat will never make a good show cat – he'll probably bite the judges! If your cat is placid and happy being handled by strangers, he may enjoy showing. Ensure he is brushed daily for at least several months before the show and this will make his coat clean and shiny. Nearer the date, lightly trim his claws and carefully clean his ears.

It's necessary to send in your show entry several months before the show date and you can find out when and where shows are to be held by consulting a cat magazine or your local newspaper.

Write to the show manager, enclosing a stamped, addressed envelope, and the manager will send you an entry form and schedule. The schedule explains everything you need to know about entering that particular show (the rules vary) and will assist you with filling in the entry form. It is very important to complete your entry form correctly, as an incorrect entry may lead to disqualification, so if you are unsure about anything, telephone the show manager and ask for an explanation.

Showing any cat is hard work – but can be great fun – especially if, at the end of the day, your cat receives a beautiful rosette to show how special he is.

November

1

2

3

4

5

6

7

8

9

10

Cats should not regularly be fed
dog food. Cats have a higher
nutrient requirement than dogs –
that's why cat food is more
expensive. For example, dog food
doesn't contain an amino acid
called taurine. Without this
nutrient in its food, a cat will go
blind.

November

11

12

13

Cats often rake open plastic
rubbish bags and eat some of the
contents, including sharp bones
which could cause internal
damage. You can dispose of
harmful rubbish safely by cutting
the top off a plastic bottle,
inserting the rubbish and pushing
the top back on firmly.

14

15

16

17

18

19

20

November

21

22

23

24

25

26

If refilling a gas lighter,
do it in a room well away
from your cat. The
hissing sound it makes is
distressing to most cats,
as a hiss is used as a sign
of aggression between
felines.

27

28

29

30

December

Christmas needn't mean extra expense as far as your cat is concerned – you can very cheaply make him a present he will love.

You can keep him happy – and save wear and tear on your furniture – by making him a scratching-post or climbing-frame. A scratching-post also provides a form of aerobic exercise for your cat, allowing him to stretch and tone up his muscles. Make one from rope wound round a table leg (ensuring no nails protrude) or carpet the treads of an old step-ladder – this will become scratching-post, climbing-frame and bed.

Your summer-grown catnip can be used to make all sorts of playthings. Two triangles of fur fabric stuffed with catnip become an interesting mouse. If you give the mouse a tail, ensure it is securely fastened or your cat may swallow it. Fur fabric tubes, four to six inches long, stuffed with catnip, are simple to make and become favourite playthings.

An even less expensive toy can be made from empty cardboard cartons. Tape the lids shut and cut holes in one or two sides and the top. If more than one box is used, glue their sides together and cut interconnecting holes between them. This sort of toy is loved by cats who will hide inside, climb in and out, and ambush one another. The boxes can be made to fit in with your decor if you paper the finished product with wallpaper.

Remember that your cat will greatly enjoy the pieces of the turkey which you won't eat – chopped-up skin, lightly-cooked giblets and the darkest meat. Do be careful that no bones are left in, as your cat will choke on these or swallow them. And why not give him a special Christmas treat – a little unflavoured cream for dessert!

December

1

2

3

4

5

December

6

7

8

9

Keep a large rush mat
just inside your front and
back doors. Many cats
love to scratch these
every time they pass. As
your cat comes in
(perhaps with dirty paws)
his mat-scratching will
wipe his feet!

10

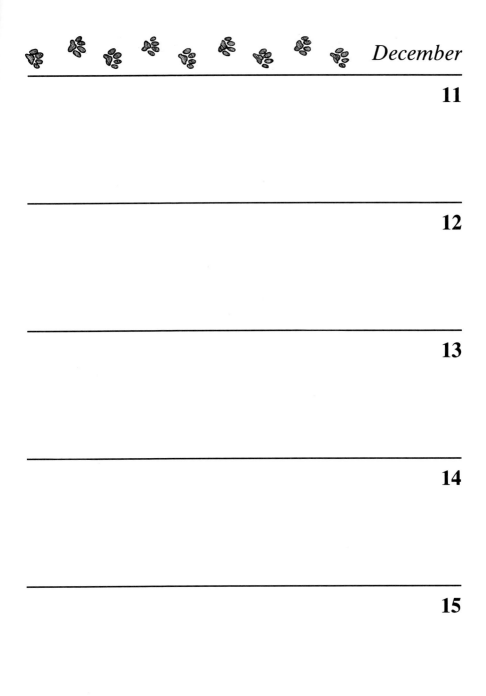

December

11

12

13

14

15

December

16

17

18

19

20

December

21

22

23

If you have a cat-loving
friend, why not buy them *The
Cat Maintenance Manual* as a
special gift. It's a book
containing hundreds of
invaluable tips and hints for cat
owners, to make their lives
easier and their cats' lives more
comfortable!

24

25

December

26

27

28

29

30

31